SUBJECT CATALOGING

A How-To-Do-It Workbook

SUBJECT CATALOGING

A How-To-Do-It Workbook

TERRY ELLEN FERL
LARRY MILLSAP

HOW-TO-DO-IT MANUALS
FOR LIBRARIES
Number 16

Series Editor: Bill Katz

NEAL-SCHUMAN PUBLISHERS, INC.
New York, London

Published by Neal-Schuman Publishers, Inc.
100 Varick Street
New York, NY 10013

Copyright © 1991 by The Regents of The University of California

All rights reserved. Reproduction of this book, in whole or in
part, without written permission of the publisher is prohibited.

Printed and bound in the United States of America

Library of Congress Cataloging-in-Publication Data

Ferl, Terry Ellen
    Subject cataloging : a how-to-do-it workbook / Terry Ellen Ferl.
Larry Millsap.
      p. cm. — (How to do it manuals for libraries ; no. 16)
    Includes bibliographical references.
    ISBN 1-55570-099-3
    1. Subject cataloging—Problems, exercises, etc. I. Millsap,
Larry. II. Title. III. Series.
Z695.F39 1991
025.4′7076—dc20   91-33045
                                                             CIP

CONTENTS

	Foreword	7
	Preface	9
1	Introduction	11
	Subject Headings	11
	Classification	13
	MARC Tagging and Coding	13
	Subject Cataloging Strategies	15
2	The Exercises	19
3	Selected Bibliography	89

FOREWORD

This workbook was developed in the University Library of the University of California, Santa Cruz at the request of MOBAC, the Monterey Bay Cooperative Library System. It is designed to help catalogers follow standard practices in assigning subject headings and call numbers. As a member of MOBAC, the library is very pleased to be able to share this knowledge with others in the library community.

Allan J. Dyson
University Librarian
UC Santa Cruz

PREFACE

This workbook is designed to give catalogers structured practice in subject cataloging. Subject cataloging in most libraries consists of two different but related tasks: assigning subject headings and assigning classification numbers to materials. Because the Library of Congress subject headings and classification system and the Dewey decimal classification system are widely used in American libraries, this workbook focuses on the principles and application of those systems.

Part I contains introductory information, and Part II contains 22 exercises with answers. Each exercise has title-page, dust-jacket, preface, and/or table of contents information for a work. The reader will assign subject headings and LC or Dewey classification numbers to the work, using the information and strategies supplied in Part I.

Most of the exercises are based on headings and numbers actually assigned to newly published materials by the Library of Congress. Some examples of works not cataloged by LC have also been included. The exercise on pages 19-20 also illustrates application of an alternative subject heading thesaurus, *Bilindex: A Bilingual Spanish-English Subject Heading List,* which contains Spanish equivalents to Library of Congress subject headings. The authors assume that the reader has access to the tools listed below.

Books are used for most of the examples, but the technique used to determine the subject of an item and then assign subject headings and call numbers is the same for materials regardless of format. Catalogers who routinely catalog specialized materials and non-book formats may wish also to consult guides on subject analysis and classification for their specialities.

There is no code for subject cataloging like the code that exists for descriptive cataloging (i.e., *AACR2*). The basic tool for assigning LC subject headings is the current edition of *Library of Congress Subject Headings (LCSH).* For assigning Library of Congress classification numbers, a combination of the Library of Congress and the Gale Research, Inc. editions of the LC classification schedules (LCC) has been used. The 20th edition of the *Dewey Decimal Classification* (DDC) and the Cutter-Sanborn 3-digit tables have been used to assign numbers in the Dewey decimal system.

An essential guide to the consistent application of LCSH is the current edition of *Subject Cataloging Manual: Subject Headings,* issued by the Library of Congress Office for Subject Cataloging Policy. An auxiliary tool that helps catalogers complete LC call numbers according to LC practice is the Library of Congress *Subject Cataloging Manual: Shelflisting.*

The *USMARC Format for Bibliographic Data* has been used for machine-readable coding of the answers to the exercises. The MARC format will be familiar to catalogers who have used a major bibliographic utility such as the OCLC Online System, or any of a variety of MARC format implementations such as *Bibliofile*.

The Library of Congress sponsored a Subject Subdivisions Conference in May 1991. Members of the library profession commented on proposals prepared by the Planning Committee and published in LC's *Cataloging Service Bulletin*. There were proposals both to limit and to expand use of subdivisions; to simplify the rules of application; to remove some information from the subject string and store it in other parts of the MARC record; and to perform an editorial cleanup of the existing LCSH system.

1 INTRODUCTION

SUBJECT HEADINGS

The goal for the cataloger assigning headings from LCSH is to apply the authorized terms to works in the same way that the Library of Congress would. LCSH contains a very useful introduction, scope notes, and extensive references that help the cataloger accomplish this to some degree. However, as the introduction to the current edition of LCSH says:

> *LCSH* . . . should be used with several auxiliary aids. Most important of these is the *Subject Cataloging Manual: Subject Headings* (the *Manual*), a third edition of which was published in 1989, and which will be updated annually. The Manual contains the same instructions used by the subject catalogers at the Library of Congress in their daily work.

This two-volume Manual, first introduced to the wider cataloging community in 1984, is perhaps the closest thing to a "code" that exists for application of LCSH. The Manual provides the cataloger with essential information on LC practice in assigning subject headings for various classes of material and on use of subdivisions. It also includes lists of subdivisions that may be used under different kinds of headings and the circumstances under which they may be used. Much of this information is not in LCSH and would not be apparent to catalogers except through examination of subject headings in LC catalog records.

The Manual contains statements of *general principles*. Section H 180 gives the *principles for assigning headings and constructing headings*. Some of those are:

> Assign to the work being cataloged one or more subject headings that best summarize the contents of the work and bring to the attention of the catalog user the most important topics discussed. Assign headings only for topics that comprise at least 20% of the work . . .

> *Specificity.* Assign headings that are as specific as the topics they cover. Assign a heading that is broader or more general than the topic to which it applies only in cases where it is not possible to establish a precise heading or in situations where an array of headings, including a general heading, is required by special instructions in the *Subject Cataloging Manual* . . .

> Subject headings may be in the form of a word, a phrase, or a name, with or without subdivisions . . . Headings assigned to a work must be complete headings containing topic and subdivision combinations in accordance with instructions in the . . . *Subject Cataloging Manual.* Special attention should be given to the instruction sheets listing free-floating subdivisions and pattern headings (H 1095-H 1200) . . .
>
> The subject headings system contains two main types of heading-subdivision combinations:
>
> a. [Place]—[topic] headings. The order usually is:
>
> [place]—[topic]—[chronological period]—[form] . . .
>
> b. [Topic]—[place] headings. The order is usually one of the following depending on whether the topical subdivision is further subdivided by place (cf. H860):
>
> [topic]—[place]—[topic]—[chronological period]—[form]
>
> *or*
>
> [topic]—[topic]—[place]—[chronological period]—[form]
>
> *Form of work.* Whenever possible within the system of LC headings and subdivisions, bring out the form of the work being cataloged by including a form subdivision in the heading . . .

Section H 180 also gives guidance on the *number of headings* to assign.

A very important matter in assigning subject headings is the use of *geographic headings and subdivisions*. The introduction to LCSH includes some information, but the cataloger will find the fullest accounts in Sections H 690-H 1050 of the Manual. There are many practices described, e.g., the formulation of headings for city districts, geographic regions, rivers, valleys, islands; the qualification of geographic headings; the construction of geographic subdivisions; exceptional treatment for specific places, e.g., Berlin, Hawaii, Washington, D.C., and so forth.

CLASSIFICATION

Once the cataloger has found subject headings that are appropriate, the headings can be used as entry points to the classification schedules. There is no current general index to the entire LC classification system. The cataloger usually has to decide which LC classification volume might be appropriate, then consult the index for that volume. There are some references between the various volumes. But, neither in LCC nor in DDC can a cataloger count on finding a reference in the index from each subject heading term to an appropriate classification number. About 40 percent of headings in LCSH are followed by LC class numbers, which generally represent the most common aspect of a subject. These, however, should be considered merely suggestive.

Generally speaking, when there is more than one subject heading chosen by the cataloger, the first subject heading must correspond to the main topic of the item, and also to the classification number chosen for the item. A cataloger may sometimes need to search the library's catalog or another database with current LC records in order to discover where items with a particular subject heading are classified in the LC or Dewey systems.

MARC TAGGING AND CODING

Subject headings are entered in a variable length *field* identified by a three-digit code called a *tag,* which is always a number in the 600s. These are referred to in the formats as the *6XXs.* Personal name headings are tagged 600; corporate name headings, 610; topical headings, 650; and geographical headings, 651. The line between topical headings, some corporate headings, and geographical headings is not always clear. Information on which tags the Library of Congress uses for problematic headings is included in Section H 405 of the Manual, in the *USMARC Format,* and is also reproduced, for example, in the OCLC format manuals. Library of Congress decisions in this matter are to some degree arbitrary, so it is necessary to have a listing of these decisions in order to make original cataloging records with tagging like that of LC. For example, names of *houses* are tagged 610, but *rooms* are tagged 650. Names of *terminal buildings* are tagged 650, names of *docks* are tagged 651. Named *ferry buildings* are tagged 650, but named *theater buildings* are tagged 610.

Two character positions called *indicators* follow each tag. These may signify the source of a heading (e.g., LCSH, or some other thesaurus), or the type of name heading (e.g., single surname, family name, jurisdiction name).

Subject-related subfield delimiters are defined for *6XX* fields as follows:

$x   General subdivision (e.g., *History*)
$y   Period subdivision (e.g., *20th century*)
$z   Place subdivision (e.g., *California*)

Some subject-related bibliographic aspects of a work are coded in the *008 Fixed-Length Data Elements Field*. This field has 40 character positions, and values have been defined for these positions. Examples of subject-related information that is coded in this field are: the nature of contents of the item; the intellectual level; whether or not the item is fiction, a conference publication, a biography, or festschrift. This coded information is not displayed to the catalog user, but it allows libraries to take advantage of a computer's capabilities to manipulate data in ways that enhance subject-related retrieval. The exercises in this workbook do not require assignment of these MARC codes, but catalogers should be aware that coding of this field may be required in the subject cataloging process.

In USMARC, fields *090-099* are now obsolete and have been reserved for local call number use and local definition. For the exercises in this workbook, we have used the OCLC input conventions for call numbers. Locally assigned LC-type call numbers are recorded in the *090* field: subfield *a* is for the class number, subfield *b* is for the Cutter number. Locally assigned Dewey call numbers are input in the *092* field, with essentially the same definitions for subfields *a* and *b*. Subfield 2 may be used to record the source (i.e., the Dewey edition number) for the class number. When there is data in subfield 2, the first indicator digit shows the nature of DDC edition information, e.g., indicator value *0* means "Full edition," and value *1* means "Abridged edition." A locally assigned Dewey call number constructed from the 20th edition would be encoded as follows:

092 0 888.0108 $b C832 $2 20

SUBJECT CATALOGING STRATEGIES

To prepare for assigning LC subject headings, a cataloger should read thoroughly the entire introduction to LCSH (about a dozen pages), and section H 180 of the Manual. It is also valuable to become familiar with the various lists of subdivisions published in the Manual.

1. Determine the subject of a work by examining the title and, if available, the dust jacket, prefatory material, and/or table of contents information. Express the subject content in words. Determining the subject of the work is the task on which every other step depends. This requires some ability to read the language of the text and to understand the subject matter, or, in the case of works of the imagination, to identify the form of the work. Determining the subject of the item requires the exercise of judgment, and catalogers do not always make the same judgment.

2. Consult LCSH under the words chosen to express the subject content. Select a used term or terms and, where appropriate, add topical, geographical, period, and/or form subdivisions, as authorized in LCSH and/or the Manual. When looking in LCSH, the cataloger should read the scope notes included with the headings, look through the lists of related terms, look through the subdivisions under the term, and scan the headings that begin with the same word. Doing so will often lead to a heading that more precisely covers the topic.

Section H 180 of the Manual says that certain topical and form subdivisions should be added to subject headings whenever appropriate. These headings are "free-floating," so are seldom printed in LCSH. The Manual contains forty separate lists of free-floating subdivisions. One may look under "Free-floating subdivisions" in the index to the Manual for access to the various categories of these subdivisions. The Library of Congress has also published *Free-floating subdivisions: An alphabetical index,* a convenient single source listing of these subdivisions, which is designed to be used in conjunction with the Manual. The cataloger should scan the appropriate lists in the Manual to see whether any terms apply to works he or she is cataloging. One quickly becomes familiar with the most common ones.

Whenever a main heading or topical subdivision may be subdivided geographically, the place name that most precisely covers the content of the book should be added following the provisions of Section H 830 of the Manual. It is also useful to remember that many subject headings consist of the place name subdivided by topic. Section H 1140 of the Manual is the listing of such subdivisions. When a topical subdivision under place also includes a period subdivision, the complete heading is printed in LCSH. These headings, for example, appear for such subdivisions as *History* or *Politics and government* under the names of countries.

3. Use the selected subject heading(s) as an entry point to the LC classification schedules. If the cataloger knows which schedule is appropriate, he or she can go directly to the index for that LC schedule and search under the subject heading chosen as the first heading. If unsure which schedule to begin with, the cataloger can use as a guide the class numbers printed with the chosen headings in LCSH. Alternatively, he or she can look in the library's catalog or another database that contains LC records, to find the class number of a recent work cataloged by LC that has the same subject heading as the first heading. (See no. 4 below for the Dewey decimal classification strategy.)

The lack of a direct link between the subject headings and classification schedules can be frustrating. As will become apparent in the examples, sometimes the subject heading term will appear in the indexes of the classification schedules but the numbers referred to will not be appropriate for the book. Other times, the term may not appear in the index at all. In many cases the cataloger will find a span of numbers in the schedule that may be appropriate and will have to use a table to complete the classification number. Lacking other direction from the schedules or the shelflisting manual, the cataloger completes the call number by adding a Cutter for the main entry and the publication date.

4. Use the subject heading(s) you have chosen as an entry point in the Relative Index to the DDC. Dewey is simpler than LC in that it has one index to the entire classification, but more complex because the number to which the index refers is seldom the complete classification number. If the term sought is not in the Relative Index, the cataloger can scan the summaries to locate the proper discipline. Once an appropriate number has been located in the schedules, it can be expanded using notation from the standard subdivisions, the general tables, or tables specific to a particular class. Additions can make the numbers very specific in the geographic area, time period, ethnic group, or kind of person related to the main topic. Tables of precedence explain the order in which one adds different numbers to express the various aspects of a topic or the aspect to prefer when only one can be expressed.

Edition 20 is the first edition of *Dewey* to include a Manual that assists in its application. The manual is very useful in building numbers and in distinguishing between similar class numbers.

The answers to the exercises in this manual include the fullest Dewey classification number that could be constructed. These are not necessarily the numbers that a library would want to use on a book. Since *Dewey* is hierarchical, digits can be dropped from the right and the number will still be correct, though less specific. To complete the call number, the cataloger adds a Cutter for the main entry. If there are two works by the same author in a class, a letter for the first word of the title is added after the Cutter for the second and all subsequent works.

2 THE EXERCISES

This section contains 22 exercises for the reader to complete, using the standard tools cited in the Preface and the strategies provided in Part 1.

Each exercise consists of two parts. The first part contains title and other information to be used as the basis for assigning subject headings and classification numbers. Each example to be worked includes the same number and type of subject heading tags as there are subject headings in the answers. The second part gives the appropriate assigned headings, classification numbers, and MARC coding, and a detailed explanation of how the data were derived.

Completion of the LC call numbers throughout the exercises is according to Sections G 060 and G 140 of *Subject Cataloging Manual: Shelflisting.* Comments are added only when departures from these guidelines are required. Completion of the Dewey call numbers is according to the Cutter-Sanborn 3-digit tables. In some exercises, the Cutter-Sanborn book numbers have been expanded according to practices described in *Book Numbers: History, Principles, and Application,* by Donald J. Lehnus (1980). To complete the call numbers, the reader will need to determine the probable main entry from the information given. In most cases, the choice of main entry will be obvious.

Tagging is not addressed in the explanations unless the particular exercise represents a departure from the MARC tagging and coding information given in Part 1 of this workbook.

EXAMPLE 1

TITLE PAGE

> # Wisdom
>
> **Its Nature, Origins, and Development**
>
> Edited by
>
> Robert J. Sternberg
>
> Cambridge : Cambridge University Press, 1990

OTHER INFORMATION

The table of contents includes:

> Part I Approaches to the study of wisdom
> Part II Approaches informed by philosophical conceptions of wisdom
> Part III Approaches informed by folk conception of wisdom
> Part IV Approaches informed by psychodevelopmental conceptions of wisdom
> Part V Integration of approaches and viewpoints

The preface includes the following paragraph:

> This book is intended for advanced undergraduates, graduate students, and professionals interested in understanding the nature of wisdom. Although the authors of the book are all psychologists, many of them draw heavily upon the philosophical literature . . . . I believe it will be indispensable reading for those wishing a broad review of current psychological thinking about wisdom.

WORKSHEET

09__

650

090   BF431 $b .W57 1990

092 0   153 $b W811 $2 20

650 0   Wisdom.

The topic of the book is wisdom from the psychologist's point of view.

Subject headings: *Wisdom* is a used term in LCSH and can be assigned as the subject heading. No subdivisions are needed.

LC Classification: In the index of *Class B: Subclass B-BJ: Philosophy, Psychology*, the entry under "Wisdom" has references to German philosophy and Renaissance philosophy. These are not appropriate to the book since the preface says that it deals with psychology rather than philosophy. Psychology is classed in BF. The outline of the class schedule for BF lists "Consciousness. Cognition. Perception. Intuition" for 309-499. A survey of these numbers reveals that the only appropriate number is BF431, "Intelligence. Mental ability. Intelligence testing. Ability testing." Wisdom is not exactly intelligence, but there is no other number that is more appropriate.

Dewey Classification: In the index, all entries under "Wisdom" lead to numbers in religion. A look through the summaries reveals that the 150s are psychology. "Intelligence, intellectual and conscious mental processes" are 153. Again, this is not exactly wisdom, but it is the most appropriate number in the psychology section.

EXAMPLE 2

TITLE PAGE

Words of Power

A Feminist Reading of the History of Logic

Andrea Nye

New York : Routledge, 1990

OTHER INFORMATION

The dust jacket includes the following:

A common complaint of philosophers, and men in general, has been that women are illogical. Women, the charge reads, contradict themselves, refuse to follow valid deductions, equivocate, and change the subject. On the other hand, rationality, defined as the ability to follow logical argument, is often claimed to be a defining characteristic of man.

Is logic masculine? Is women's lack of interest in the "hard core" philosophical disciplines of formal logic and semantics symptomatic of an inadequacy linked to sex? Is the failure of women to excel in pure mathematics and mathematical science a function of their inability to think rationally?

Andrea Nye undermines the assumptions that inform these questions, assumptions such as: logic is unitary, logic is independent of concrete human relations, logic transcends historical circumstances as well as gender. In a series of studies of the logics of historical figures—Parmenides, Plato, Aristotle, Zeno, Abelard, Ockham, and Frege—she traces the changing interrelationships between logical innovation and oppressive speech strategies, showing that logic is not transcendent truth but abstract forms of language spoken by men, whether Greek ruling citizens, imperial administrators, church officials, or scientists. She relates logical techniques, such as logical division, syllogisms, and truth functions, to ways in which those with power speak to and about those subject to them. She shows, in the specific historical settings of Ancient and Hellenistic Greece, medieval Europe, and Germany between the World Wars, how logicians reworked language so that dialogue and reciprocity are impossible and one speaker is forced to accept the words of another.

The question then is not whether women can do logic but whether they have been willing to use "words of power" to silence others. Even more important, does such a refusal condemn them to powerlessness?

WORKSHEET

09__

650

650

090   BC57 $b .N94 1990

092 0   160.82 $b N994 $2 20

650 0   Logic $x History.

650 0   Feminism $x Philosophy.

The topic of the book is the history of logic from a feminist perspective.

Subject headings: LCSH includes the heading *Logic*. The list of free-floating subdivisions in the Manual includes *History*; so that should be added. However, the relationship to feminism requires a second heading. There are no headings for Feminist philosophy or Feminism and philosophy. *Philosophy* is a free-floating subdivision included in Section H 1095 of the Manual. It can be added to the heading *Feminism*, and that is as close to the topic as one can get. This is an example of two headings which individually are broader in scope than the subject of the book, but which together provide specific coverage.

LC Classification: LCSH includes a reference to schedule BC with the heading Logic. In *Class B: Subclasses B-BJ: Philosophy, Psychology* there is a section under Logic for "Philosophy, Methodology, Relationships to other topics." A list of several specific topics is followed by provision for non-specified "Other" in BC57. Since the book deals with the relationship of logic to feminism and feminism is not included in the list of topics, it should be classified in BC57.

Dewey Classification: The term "Logic (Reasoning)" in the index refers to 160. The relationship of women to the topic can be shown by the addition of the standard subdivision -082. Since the main number ends in 0, the 0 is dropped from the subdivision.

EXAMPLE 3

TITLE PAGE

> # Modern First Ladies
>
> ## Their Documentary Legacy
>
> Compiled and Edited by
>
> Nancy Kegan Smith and Mary C. Ryan
>
> Washington, D.C.: National Archives and Records Administration, 1989

OTHER INFORMATION

The foreword states that:

> [This book is] an exploration of the records of first ladies . . . . In some instances, the Social Files [which form a portion of the] . . . repositories [in the presidential libraries] contain thousands of boxes of documents and letters that disclose how individual first ladies functioned and how the American public responded to their work . . . . This book is an endeavor to show what presidential libraries can offer to the interested scholar and writer . . . in an effort to penetrate . . . "the veil of mystery" that has surrounded women who have added much to the record of American history in this century.

WORKSHEET

09__

650

```
090      CD3029.82 $b M63 1989

092 0    973.90922 $b M689 $2 20

650 0    Presidents $z United States $x Wives $x Archives.
```

This book of essays discusses the documentary material on Twentieth Century United States presidents' wives, which is to be found in the various presidential libraries.

Subject Headings: There is a cross reference in LCSH from *First ladies (United States)* to *Presidents—United States—Wives*. It is appropriate to add the free-floating form subdivision *Archives* to this subject heading. Since less than 50 percent of this book deals with personal aspects of the lives of presidential wives, it is not considered a collective biography and so does not merit a subject added entry of the type *[Class of persons]—Biography* prescribed in Section H 1330 of the Manual.

LC Classification: LCSH has no suggested number for this subject heading. The index to *Class E-F: History: America* lists "Presidents (U.S.)...Biography...Wives: E176.2." But, as stated above, this work does not qualify as a collective biography. LCSH has a cross reference from *Presidential libraries* to *Presidents—United States—Archives*, but no class number is suggested. In LCSH, under *Archives*, the CD class is recommended. The index to *Class C: Auxiliary Sciences of History* lists "Presidential libraries (United States): CD3029.82".

Dewey Classification: The subject of this collection is the archival material of the presidential wives, so the appropriate discipline is history, which is included in the 900 class. Searching the index under "Presidents" and "Wives" is not productive in this case, but under "History" we find "specific places, 930-990." The history of the United States in the Twentieth Century is readily found under 973.9 in the schedule, which provides a chronological approach. This number is expanded by adding 0922 for "Persons, Collected treatment" from Table 1, Standard Subdivisions. The note in the schedule prescribes 092 for "Biography, autobiography, description and critical appraisal of work, diaries, reminiscences, correspondence of persons regardless of area, region, place..."

EXAMPLE 4

TITLE PAGE

Cultures in Contact

The Impact of European Contacts on Native American Cultural Institutions

A.D. 1000 - 1800

Edited & with commentary by

William W. Fitzhugh

OTHER INFORMATION

The following information is from the table of contents:

Part I. The Arctic sector: Inuit responses to explorers, whalers, traders, and missionaries.

Early contacts north of Newfoundland before A.D. 1600.
European goods and socio-economic change in early Labrador Inuit society.
Whales, whalers, and Eskimos: The impact of European whaling on the demography and economy of Eskimo society in west Greenland.

Part II. New England—the move inland: land, politics, and disease.

Preliminary biocultural interpretations from a Seventeenth-century Narragansett Indian cemetery in Rhode Island.
Cultural change on the southern New England frontier, 1630-1665.
New York Iroquois political development.

Part III. The Chesapeake: two views—anthropology and history.

Socio-political organization within the Powhatan chiefdom and the effects of European contact, A.D. 1607-1634.
Patterns of Anglo-Indian aggression and accommodation along the Mid-Atlantic coast, 1584-1634.

Part IV. The South—labor, tribute, and social policy: the Spanish legacy.

Spanish-Indian interaction in Sixteenth-century Florida and Hispaniola.

WORKSHEET   09__

650

650

650

650

090		E98.C89 $b C74 1985
092	0	973.0497 $b C968 $2 20
650	0	Indians of North America $x Cultural assimilation.
650	0	Indians of North America $x History $y Colonial period, ca. 1600-1775.
650	0	Indians of North America $x First contact with Occidental civilization.
650	0	Indians of North America $x Foreign influences.

This book is about Native Americans along the Atlantic seaboard from A.D. 1000 to 1800, and the influence of European contacts on their cultures. About half of the book deals with Native Americans in the American colonies.

Subject Headings: In LCSH, under *Native Americans,* one finds the reference *USE Indians of North America*. The cataloger scans the list of subdivisions under this heading, searching for one to express the concept of contact with Europeans or cultural influence of Europeans. One finds the used subdivision *Chinese influences,* which suggests that one might also find the used subdivision *European influences*. However, the latter is not in the list. One then finds the used subdivision *Cultural assimilation,* which does express a central topic of this book. Next, one finds this directive under *Indians of North America—Culture*:

> USE subdivision Chinese, [Egyptian], Transpacific, etc.] influences
>   under *Indians of North America* for specific foreign influences
>   on the culture of Indians of North America
>
> Indians of North America
> Indians of North America—Foreign influences

Since there is no subdivision for *European influences,* the cataloger selects the broader term *Indians of North America—Foreign influences* to cover this aspect of the book's content. It is clear at this point that no single heading will cover the theme of this book. Continuing to scan the list of subdivisions, one finds *First contact with Occidental civilization*. This heading is also appropriate for this book. Parts II and III of the book deal more specifically with the American colonial period. Under *Indians of North America—History,* one finds the period subdivision *Colonial period, ca. 1600-1775*. Among the four headings selected, the heading *Indians of North America—Cultural assimilation* is the most comprehensive, and therefore becomes the entry point for selecting a classification number.

LC Classification: In LCSH, there is no LC class number printed with the most comprehensive heading for this book. Under *Indians of North America,* however, E77-99 is suggested. The index to *Class E-F: History: America* has a series of listings under "Indians," one of which is "Indians: North America: E77-99." In the same index, under "Cultural assimilation," one finds "Cultural assimilation, Indian: E98.C89; F1525.3.C84, F2519.3.C85, etc." The first number turns out to be the correct one. In the schedule, it is for "Indians of North America: Other topics, A-Z . . . .C89 Cultural assimilation."

Dewey Classification: The index lists "Indians of North America T5-97." This tells us that materials about these peoples will be classified under the appropriate discipline (e.g., historical works in the 900 class, works on art in the 700 class). The appropriate discipline for this book is history, and the area is North America. In the schedule, the "Summary" under 970, General History of North America, lists 973 for the United States. To this number, we add from Table 1 the number .04 ("Special topics"), then the number 97 (for Indians of North America) from Table 5. Note that the DDC's dispersed classification of materials on North American Indians contrasts with LC's assignment of most of those materials to class E77-99.

EXAMPLE 5

TITLE PAGE

Between Borders

Essays on Mexican/Chicana History

Edited by

Adelaida R. Del Castillo

Encina, CA : Floricanto Press, © 1990

OTHER INFORMATION

Text from the back cover:

> A remarkable anthology of original research and interpretive essays on the history of the Mexicana/Chicana. Collected here are twenty-five essays by an international group of scholars who discuss methods, content and critical theoretical concerns of Chicana historiography to date. Together these writings comprise an unprecedented collection of studies on Mexican women in the United States.

The essays are in English or Spanish.

WORKSHEET

09__

650

650

```
090      E184.M5 $b B4 1990

092 0    305.486872 $b B565 $2 20

650 0    Mexican American women $x History.

650 0    Women $z Mexico $x History.

650 7    Mujeres mexicano-americanas $x Historia. $2 bidex

650 7    Mujeres $z Mexico $x Historia. $2 bidex
```

The subject of this book is the history of Mexicanas and Chicanas or, in English, Mexican women and Mexican American women.

LC Subject Headings: LCSH is an English-language list; so it is necessary to approach it using English terms rather than Mexicanas and Chicanas. There is a heading *Chicanos*, but it refers to *Mexican Americans*. Under the heading *Mexican Americans*, there is a subdivision *Women*, that refers to *Mexican American women*. The heading may be subdivided by place. However the coverage is not limited to a particular state or section of the country, and *Mexican American women—United States* is a redundancy. So no geographic subdivision is used. *Mexican women* does not appear in LCSH, but the heading *Women* does and can be subdivided geographically. The free-floating subdivision *History* is appropriate to both these headings.

Since some libraries find it useful to include Spanish-language headings to guide Spanish-speaking users to materials in their own language, also included here are headings from *Bilindex : a bilingual Spanish-English subject heading list : Spanish equivalents to Library of Congress Subject Headings*. Since these are not LC subject headings, the second indicator digit is 7 and the source of the heading is specified in subfield 2.

LC Classification: In the index of *Class H: Subclasses HM-HX: Social Sciences: Sociology* there is no entry for "Women," but "Woman" refers to class HQ. A survey of the HQ schedule reveals that books on the history of women in a particular place are classed in HQ1410-1870.5. The index of *Class E-F: History: America* refers from "Mexicans in the United States" to E184.M5. So the cataloger is faced with choosing between two numbers, each of which is broader than the topic of the book. Consulting a subject catalog of LC records shows that E184 is the number that is preferred.

Dewey Classification: In the index "Women" refers to 305.4, which is part of "Social groups." The table of precedence at the beginning of this section says that divisions by sex take precedence over divisions by racial or ethnic group. The number is to be added to as is the number for men,

305.3. Under "Men" the cataloger is directed to add from Table 5 to 305.38 for racial, ethnic, or national groups. In Table 5, -687-688 is for Spanish America. The number can be expanded from the geographic area tables for specific countries; so -6872 is used for Mexico. That number is added to 305.48, the parallel number for women.

THE EXERCISES **37**

EXAMPLE 6

TITLE PAGE

> # They Saw the Elephant
>
> ## Women in the California Gold Rush
>
> Joanne Levy
>
> Hamden, Ct. : Archon Books, 1990

OTHER INFORMATION

Text from the dust jacket:

> Here is a medley of the voices of pioneer women, telling how they trekked by the thousands to gold rush California. Crossing the Isthmus of Panama on the backs of mules, inching their way across Great American Desert in prairie schooners, they braved the unknown with great courage and daring. Some women followed their husbands, fathers, brothers, or lovers; others made their way alone, by their own choice.
>
> Countless letters, diaries, and reminiscences survive to testify to their feelings and their achievements, to their experiences coping with adversity—and the freedom—they found at the frontier. In their own words they tell us how they laid another child to rest along the way, encountered Indians, thirsted under the merciless desert sun, and stepped out of their burdensome layers of petticoats to do whatever needed to be done.
>
> Women established homes in the towns and camps, some mining for gold themselves, others setting up businesses to earn it with their domestic skills. Women were gamblers, actresses, missionaries, church builders, innkeepers, school teachers, prostitutes—one was even a stagecoach driver with Wells, Fargo & Co. Women worked at every occupation and lived in every quarter of society. There was no stage in the development of the West that did not feel their presence.

WORKSHEET

```
09__
651
650
650
650
```

```
090       F865 $b .L67 1990

092 0     979.404082 $b L668 $2 20

651 0     California $x Gold discoveries.

650 0     Women pioneers $z California $x History $y 19th century.

650 0     Women $z California $x History $y 19th century.

650 0     Frontier and pioneer life $z California.
```

The subject of this book is the California gold rush and women's relationship to it. There is description of life on the frontier.

Subject headings: Gold rush is the central topic. It can be found in LCSH as a reference to *Gold mines and mining*. Under that heading is a see also reference to the subdivision *Gold discoveries* under names of countries. Section H 1140 of the Manual provides the information that the subdivision can also be used under states; so the heading *California—Gold discoveries* covers the topic of the gold rush. There is no subdivision that adds the relationship of women to the topic; so it must be covered by separate headings. The headings *Women pioneers* and simply *Women* are included in LCSH. *Women pioneers* is appropriate to many of the women, but probably not all of them; so both are used. Both can be subdivided geographically. According to Section H 830 of the Manual, the first element of a geographical subdivision is the name of a country. However, the Manual also provides for exceptional treatment for Canada, Great Britain, the Soviet Union, and the United States. The first order political divisions of these countries may be assigned directly. So States of the United States can be the first element in a geographical subdivision, as California is in these headings. Since geographic subdivisions can have only two levels, the necessity for these exceptions is readily apparent. Section H 1100 of the Manual gives the general subdivisions that can be used under classes of persons. The one appropriate to this book is *History—19th century*. A final subject heading is added to cover the aspect of frontier life in a particular place. It is *Frontier and pioneer life*, also a heading that can be subdivided geographically.

LC Classification: In the index of *Class E-F: History: America*, the term "California—Gold discoveries" leads to F865. In the schedule, the coverage of F865 is given as California history from 1848-1856. The classification can cover only the major topic of the book.

Dewey Classification: In the index under "California" there is a reference to 979.4. In the schedules is an historical table, and .404 is used for the period 1848-1899. To this can be added the standard subdivision -082 which is to show the relationship of women to a subject. So the Dewey classification can more precisely describe the topic of the book than can the LC classification.

EXAMPLE 7

TITLE PAGE

> # The Defeat of Che Guevara
>
> ## Military Response to Guerrilla Challenge in Bolivia
>
> Gary Prado Salmon
> Translated by John Deredita
>
> New York : Praeger, 1990

OTHER INFORMATION

The dust jacket includes the following information:

> A thoroughly documented account of the 1967 guerrilla challenge in Bolivia, *The Defeat of Che Guevara* reconstructs events leading up to, during, and after the defeat of the insurgency. Against the background of the 1960s' attempt to extend Cuban influence throughout Latin America, the book provides an analysis of trends in Bolivian politics from 1952 to 1967. General Gary Prado Salmon evaluates the geographical setting of the insurgency, guerrilla preparations, and the Bolivian response. He identifies key strategic errors, including Che Guevara's failure to capture peasant support, and analyzes Che's own theories.

Text from the Foreword includes:

> Prado's detailed and generally objective analysis of the campaign is unmatched for its clarity and balance. His observations on the shortcomings of both the army and the guerrillas are honest and accurate and dramatically detail Che's failures against poorly prepared troops . . . . Although one may disagree with some of Prado's introductory comments and historical interpretations of U.S. policies and actions in Latin America, it is difficult to fault his analysis of the Bolivian Army's reaction to the guerrilla threat . . . . His study benefits not only from his participation as commander of the unit that finally captured Guevara, but also from his familiarity with the region where the action took place.

WORKSHEET

09__
651
600
650
610
650

090   F3326 $b .P7313 1990

092 0   984.05 $b P896Z261 $2 20

651 0   Bolivia $x History $y 1938-1982.

600 10   Guevara, Ernesto, $d 1926-1967.

650 0   Guerrillas $z Bolivia $x History $y 20th century.

610 10   Bolivia. $b Ejercito $x Commando troops $x History $y 20th century.

650 0   Bolivia $x History, Military.

The central topic of this book is a detailed account of the Bolivian army's defeat of the guerrilla insurgency in Bolivia led by Che Guevara.

Subject Headings: This book is primarily about a particular period in Bolivia's history and so should have a subject heading for that. In LCSH, *Bolivia* is a used term, with the subdivision *History*, further divided by the period subdivision *1938-1982*. A subject entry for Che Guevara is appropriate because Section H 180 of the Manual says to "assign headings for individual persons, families, corporate bodies, projects, places, etc., significant for the work as a whole, even if discussion of these entities does not form 20% of the work being cataloged." The form for his name as a subject is found in the *LC Name Authorities*. Since a considerable portion of the book is devoted to an account of the conflict between the insurgency forces and the Bolivian army forces, headings should be added to cover these groups. *Guerrillas* is a used term and may be subdivided geographically. The specific historical period should be brought out in this heading and the heading described immediately below. According to Section H 1647 of the Manual, *History—[century]* subdivisions are free-floating and should be assigned whenever it is possible to do so, provided there are no contrary provisions in LCSH.

A heading is needed for the Bolivian army troops that fought the insurgency. In LCSH under *Armies,* there is a see also reference to *names of individual armies, e.g. United States. Army*. This type of heading is a corporate body heading and would be tagged 610 when used as a subject. While *Bolivia* does appear in LCSH, there is no subdivision for the name of Bolivia's army. Under "Armed forces" in the index to the Manual, there is a reference to the pattern heading for military services, which appears in Section H 1159. *United States. Army* is the pattern heading. The cataloger must consult the *LC Name Authorities* to find the established form of the name for the army of Bolivia, i.e., *Bolivia. Ejercito*. Under *Counterinsurgency,* a used term in LCSH, one finds the narrower term *Commando troops*. Under this heading, there is a see also note instructing one to use the term as a *subdivision under names of individual military services, e.g. United States. Army—Commando troops.* This provides the pattern for the heading for the Bolivian army. The subdivisions *History—20th century* are then added.

This work is also, of course, a military history. In LCSH under *Military history,* there is a see also reference to the *subdivision History, Military under names of countries, cities, etc.*

LC Classification: This book is readily classified by looking under "Bolivia" in the index to *Class E-F: History. America.* Books on the history of Bolivia for the period that includes the 1967 insurgency are classified in F3326, which covers the period 1938-1982. Since this work is a translation, the Cutter number for the book is expanded, in accord with the Translation Table in Section G 150 of the Manual. LC uses this table only when a uniform title plus language(s) is provided in the description of the item, and when the main entry is a personal author or title. In this case, the LC descriptive cataloging record contains a uniform title,

    240 10 Guerrilla inmolada. $l English

so the designation ".x13 English translation" from the Translation Table is appropriate. The ".x" signifies the first part of the cutter number (in this case .P73, for the main entry "Prado Salmon, Gary"), to which one adds "13".

Dewey Classification: The subject of the book is Bolivia and the discipline is History. The index lists "Bolivia 984." In the schedule, there is provision for three chronological periods: 1899-, 1899-1952, and 1952-. The most inclusive number is used to match the full range of information covered by the book. Following the Cutter number for the author's compound surname, a second Cutter is added because the work is a translation. This number is formed from tables published in Donald Lehnus's *Book Numbers.*

EXAMPLE 8

TITLE PAGE

Portrait Gallery

Agnes De Mille

Boston : Houghton Mifflin, 1990

OTHER INFORMATION

Text from the dust jacket:

> Not only is Agnes de Mille one of our most distinguished choreographers, creator of such ballets as *Rodeo, Fall River Legend,* and *The Informer* as well as the famous dances of musical shows ranging from *Oklahoma!* to *Brigadoon,* but she has written twelve previous books recording her experience in the dance and the theater. *Portrait Gallery,* her thirteenth and most vivid, brings to life (or back to life) people she has known on the stage, behind the curtain, and in the intimacies of her private life.

The table of contents includes:

    I. Artists
        Isadora Duncan, Alicia Markova, Katherine Dunham, Carmelita Maracci, Alicia Alonso
    II. Impresarios
        The Shuberts, Billy Rose, The Marquis de Cuevas, The Last Impresario
    III. The De Milles
    IV. Intimates
        The Giver of Parties, Allie: All for Love, Cornelia, Avoir du Cran, Old New York

WORKSHEET

09__

600

650

650

650

```
090       GV1785.D36  $b  A3  1990

092  0    792.8092  $b  D381ap  $2  20

600  10   De Mille, Agnes.

650  0    Dancers $z United States $x Biography.

650  0    Choreographers $z United States $x Biography.

600  10   De Mille, Agnes $x Friends and associates.
```

This is a work by an American dancer, recounting her experiences in the dance and in the theater.

Subject Headings: This book meets the definition in Section H 1330 of the Manual for biography and autobiography: "A narrative work more than 50% of which recounts the personal aspects of the life of one or more individuals . . . " A subject heading for the biographee (in this case the author) is added. The form for De Mille's name as a subject is found in *LC Name Authorities*. The subdivision *Biography* is not added to her name. Instead, the Manual prescribes a heading of the type *[Class of persons]—Biography* when such headings exist. Since De Mille is described as a dancer and a choreographer, subject headings for both of these used terms are added. The geographical subdivision *United States* is inserted before the form subdivision *Biography,* in accord with Section H 180 of the Manual. Though the various persons described in De Mille's book are quite famous, subject headings are not made for any of them. Recall the general principle in Section H 180 of the Manual: "Assign headings only for topics that comprise at least 20% of the work." Section H 1110 of the Manual contains a list of free-floating subdivisions for use under names of persons. The subdivision *Friends and associates* is used "for discussions of the person's close and immediate contacts such as companions, co-workers, etc." This subdivision, added to the subject heading for De Mille, will cover the many relationships De Mille describes.

LC Classification: LCSH does not suggest a class number under *Dancers,* but does give GV1785 under *Choreographers*. The index to *Class G: Geography; Maps; Anthropology; Recreation* lists "Dancers: GV1785." In the schedule, that number is divided further by Cutter numbers for individual dancers, A-Z, and examples are given for numbers already assigned. The cataloger should determine whether LC has already assigned a Cutter number for De Mille. This may be done by searching the library's catalog or some other available database that includes LC records. LC has already used D36 for De Mille. The

Biography Table in Section G 320 of the Manual lists "A3: Autobiography, diaries, etc. By date."

Dewey Classification: The index lists "Autobiographies 920, T1-092." The note under 920 in the schedule says to "class biography of persons associated with a specific discipline or subject with the discipline or subject, using notation 092 from Table 1."

Other options for classifying biographies and autobiographies are suggested in the schedule, for example, classing all individual biographies in 92. However, LC follows the directive quoted above and classes this work in the DDC number for "Ballet and modern dance," 792.8. This number is listed in the index both under "Dancers" and "Modern dance." To this number we need only to add 092 from Table 1. The work letter "a" is added to the cutter number for this autobiography. An additional letter "p" is added for the title of the work, because this is the thirteenth such work by the author.

EXAMPLE 9

TITLE PAGE

> # Jump Start
>
> ## Japan Comes to the Heartland
>
> David Gelsanliter
>
> New York : Farrar, Straus, Giroux, 1990

OTHER INFORMATION

Text from the dust jacket includes:

> [An] ... investigation of the American operations of the three leading Japanese automobile manufacturers and their stunning effectiveness in winning over the American work force .... With a fiction writer's eye for detail, anecdote, and personality, Gelsanliter has followed Honda, Nissan, and Toyota as they penetrate—economically, politically, and socially—into the fabric of our heartland communities. Working carefully and diplomatically from its base plant in Marysville, Ohio, Honda has quietly increased its presence in American manufacturing to where it is now about to surpass Chrysler .... Nissan's American management teams in Tennessee and the more established Toyota organization in Georgetown, Kentucky, have adjusted to the American Midwest ... in ways equally subtle and profound .... The Japanese ... have been largely successful at inspiring their American employees to adopt Japanese ideals of long-term loyalty and a team-oriented company ethic.

WORKSHEET

09__

650

650

650

090		HD9710.U62 $b G45 1990
092	0	338.8872920973 $b G321 $2 20
650	0	Automobile industry and trade $z United States.
650	0	Corporations, Japanese $z United States.
650	0	Automobile industry workers $z United States $x Attitudes.

The topic of this book is the operations of the three leading Japanese auto manufacturing companies in plants located in the United States, and the attitudes of the American employees at those plants.

Subject Headings: LCSH lists *Automobiles* as a used term. Under this term, there is a *see also* reference to "headings beginning with the word *Automobile*". Scanning that part of LCSH, one finds *Automobile industry and trade,* which seems appropriate to cover the operations of the plants. This phrase may be subdivided geographically. One would not want to subdivide it by *Japan,* because the book deals with plants located in the United States, not with those located in Japan. There is no subdivision that can be added to bring out the connection of the Japanese companies with the American automobile industry.

Next, one seeks a term that will cover the Japanese auto companies. One might search LCSH under the term *Companies,* in an effort to get to a heading dealing with Japanese companies. LCSH refers one from *Companies* to three possible headings: *Business enterprises; Corporations;* or *Partnerships.* Under *Corporations,* one may scan the list and find *Corporations, American, [French, etc.],* which is used for "works on foreign corporations chartered by nationals of individual countries." One also sees, further along in LCSH, the used term *Corporations, Japanese,* which may be subdivided geographically.

A search in LCSH under *Auto workers* or *automobile workers* leads to the used term *Automobile industry workers,* which may be subdivided geographically. The index to the Manual lists "Classes of persons . . . Free-floating subdivisions under: H 1100." There one finds the subdivision *Attitudes,* which is appropriate to add to the heading for the automobile workers. There is no heading that covers the influence of Japanese ideals on workers from another culture.

LC Classification: LCSH suggests the TL class under the heading *Automobiles.* But the index to that schedule lists nothing about the automobile industry. *Class T: Technology* is not appropriate because this book is about the industry or business side of automobile manufacturing. In *Class H: Subclasses H-HJ: Social Sciences: Economics,* one finds "Automobile industry: HD9710+" in the index. This number, which is appropriate for the book, appears in the schedule as follows:

```
HD
      Special industries and trades
          Mechanical industries . . .
              Automobiles. Motor vehicles . . .
 9710             General works
```

The footnote, which appears for each industry group, says:

For subarrangement, *see* tables following HD9999

These tables provide different treatment for different industries, depending on whether a Cutter number, one number, 11 numbers, or 20 numbers have been assigned to an industry. For example, the iron and steel industry has been assigned the range of numbers HD9510-9529, so "Table A (20 nos.)" applies. The automobile industry has only one number, HD9710, so "Table C (One number)" should be used. Table C allows the cataloger to subarrange as follows:

```
.A4-Z          By region or country, A-Z
```

The Cutter number for the United States should be taken from the table at the end of the *H-HJ* schedule, "List of Regions and Countries in One Alphabet." This table assigns ".U6" for the United States. Table C then directs the cataloger to add to the region or country number the digit "2" for "General works. History." In the designation ".x2" in Table C, the ".x" signifies whichever region or country number applies. So, in this case we use .U62. (Whenever a particular LC schedule does not have its own region or country table, the cataloger should consult the table in section G 300 of the Manual.) The call number is completed with a final Cutter number for the main entry, plus the year of publication, in accord with G 060 and G 140 of the Manual.

Dewey Classification: The index contains the entry "Automobiles, production economics 338.476 292 22," which suggests the appropriate discipline Economics. Our book is on two subjects, so we will classify it with the one judged to receive fuller treatment, i.e., Japanese auto companies operating in the United States. In scanning the schedules under 338, we find that .887 is for multinational business enterprises in specific industries. The range of numbers .8872-.8879 applies to manufacturing. The note says to "add to the base number 338.887 the numbers following 6 in 620-690" of the schedules. The "Summary" under "620 Engineering and allied operations" lists 629.2 for motor land vehicles. To this number, 338.887292, we then add 09 from Table 1 for the standard subdivision "geographical location," plus 73 from Table 2 for the United States.

EXAMPLE 10

TITLE PAGE

Drinking and Driving

Advances in Research and Prevention

Edited by

R. Jean Wilson
Robert E. Mann

New York : Guilford Press, © 1990

OTHER INFORMATION

Text from the dust jacket includes:

> This is an invaluable resource for people interested in the current status of the drinking-driving problem. For the first time, the major divergent lines of research and theory on drinking and driving are brought together and integrated under one cover, making this book an authoritative reference for anyone concerned with traffic safety and alcohol abuse.

The table of contents includes:

> Part I. Understanding the Impaired Driver
> Part II. Deterrence and the Drinking-Driving Problem
> Part III. Other Preventive Approaches

WORKSHEET

09__

650

650

```
090      HE5620.D7 $b D75 1990

092 0    363.1257 $b D795 $2 20

650 0    Drunk driving $x Prevention.

650 0    Drinking and traffic accidents.
```

The topic of this book is drunk driving and its prevention.

Subject Headings: LCSH has a single term that covers the main topic of this book, i.e. *Drunk driving*. One can find this readily by looking under the words *Drinking,* or *Driving,* or *Drunk*. Under the word *Driving,* there is a reference from the unused term *Driving under the influence of alcohol* to the used term *Drunk driving*. This book deals with the prevention of drunk driving. Looking under *Prevention* in LCSH does not give you a heading related to drunk driving, but Section H 1095 of the Manual lists *Prevention* as a free-floating subdivision of general application that may be used under "individual or types of diseases and medical conditions, and under situations to be avoided." So it is appropriate to add it to our main heading. Under *Drunk driving,* the scope note in LCSH says that "works on the relation between alcoholic intoxication and traffic accidents are entered under *Drinking and traffic accidents,*" so this heading will also be added.

LC Classification: LCSH does not suggest a class number for the heading *Drunk driving,* but does suggest HE5620.D7 for use with *Drinking and traffic accidents*. The index to *Class H: Subclasses H-HJ: Social Sciences: Economics* does list "Drunken driving: HE5620.D7," the appropriate number for this book.

Dewey Classification: The index lists "Drunk driving, causes of accidents, 363.125 1." In the schedule, this number is for "Highway and urban vehicular transportation, causes of accidents." The associated footnote refers the cataloger to instructions under 362-363, where an additional table of digits is printed. Our book focuses on the *prevention* of drunk driving, so instead of adding the digit 1 to 363.125 for "social causes", we add 7, for "measures to prevent, protect against, limit effects of problems."

EXAMPLE 11

TITLE PAGE

> # Writing Winning Proposals With Your PC
>
> **Herman Holtz**
>
> Glenview, Illinois : Scott Foresman and Company, 1990

OTHER INFORMATION

Text from the preface includes:

Proposal writing may be the most important activity in your career track. That is one of the premises upon which this book is based. I anticipate that some readers will be new to the art of proposal writing, while others will be thoroughly expert in the art, and I have therefore tried to provide for both readers by dividing the book into two sections.

Section 1 is a virtual primer in proposal writing, presenting the basics of the subject. Section 2 explores and explains the many contributions made by the PC when it is used effectively.

For an increasing number of businesses, proposal writing is as essential to life as water and air are to human life.

WORKSHEET

09__

650

650

```
090       HF5718.5 $b .H65 1990

092 0     808.066658 $b H758 $2 20

650 0     Proposal writing in business $x Data processing.

650 0     Microcomputers.
```

The topic of the book is proposal writing using a PC in a business setting.

Subject Headings: In LCSH there are a series of headings beginning *Proposal writing in*, the first one being *Proposal writing in business*. That heading matches some of the content of the book but does not include the idea of using a PC. There is, however, a free-floating subdivision in section H 1095 of the Manual available for adding the concept of computer applications to other headings. It is the subdivision *Data processing*. That heading does not specifically cover the idea of PCs; so another heading is necessary to cover that aspect. There is no entry for *PC* in LCSH. Under *Personal computers* there is a reference to *Microcomputers*.

LC Classification: In determining the classification, one must determine whether in the classification system being used writing is an aspect of business or business is an aspect of writing. In the index of *Class H: Subclasses H-HJ: Social Sciences: Economics*, "Proposal writing (Business communication)" refers to HF5718.5. This is the appropriate number for this work.

Dewey Classification: In the Dewey index there are no entries under "Proposal writing," "Business writing," or "Writing, Business." If one checks a subject catalog under the heading "Proposal writing . . .," all books have the Dewey number 808.066. That is the number for Technical writing. The cataloger adds a three-digit number 001-999 for the specific subject. Dewey has no number for "Business"; the number 658 is for "General management."

EXAMPLE 12

TITLE PAGE

> # Coping with City Growth During the British Industrial Revolution
>
> by Jeffrey G. Williamson
>
> Cambridge : Cambridge University Press, 1990

OTHER INFORMATION

From the table of contents:

1 Coping with city growth, past and present
2 The urban demographic transition: Births, deaths, and immigration
3 Migrant selectivity, brain drain, and human capital transfers
4 The demand for labor and immigrant absorption off the farm
5 Absorbing the city immigrants
6 The impact of the Irish on British labor markets
7 Did British labor markets fail during the industrial revolution?
8 Did Britain's cities grow too fast?
9 City housing, density, disamenities, and death

Text from the dust jacket includes:

Coping with City Growth assesses British performance with city growth during the First Industrial Revolution by combining the tools used by Third World analysts with the archival attention and eclectic style of the economic historian. What emerges is an exciting and provocative new account of a very old problem.

A selection from page seven of the text reads as follows:

"Urbanization did not outpace industrialization during the First Industrial Revolution. Furthermore it appears that the demand for labor in the cities was fairly elastic and shifted to the right at very buoyant rates during the four critical decades, 1821-1861, when city growth problems were said to have reached their peak."

WORKSHEET

09__

650

651

090		HT384.G7 b W54 1990
092	0	307.76094109034 $b W729 $2 20
650	0	Cities and towns $z Great Britain $x Growth $x History $y 19th century.
651	0	Great Britain $x Economic conditions $y 1760-1860.

The topic of the book is the growth of cities in Britain during the Industrial Revolution and the economic conditions that led to the growth.

Subject Headings: When a cataloger looks for the term *Cities* in LCSH, he or she will find that the used heading is *Cities and towns*. The term can be subdivided geographically and there is also a subdivision *Growth*. When the main heading says (May subd geog) and the topical subdivision does not, the geographical subdivision comes between the main heading and the topical subdivision. The authorized name for Britain, *Great Britain*, is found in *LC Name Authorities*. There is no subdivision to express the concept of coping, but there are ones available to describe the period of time that is being covered. The free floating subdivisions in Section H 1095 of the Manual include *History—19th century*. Since the book also includes information on the economic history of Britain, a second heading is added to cover that. LSCH includes a see also reference from *Economic history* to the subdivision *Economic conditions* used under names of places. This aspect of the topic is then covered by the heading *Great Britain—Economic conditions*. There are two period subdivisions for the heading that could be appropriate: *1760-1860* and *19th century*. Since 1820-1860 is covered by both subdivisions, a search in a database with LC records is required to reveal that the former is used to describe works on the Industrial Revolution. The table of contents shows that many specific aspects of the economic history of the period are covered in this book. Since no one of them makes up more than twenty per cent of it, the general heading is used to cover them all.

LC Classification: In LCSH there is a reference to HT371 for city problems under the heading *Cities and towns—Growth*. If the cataloger begins there in *Class H: Subclasses HM-HX: Social Sciences: Sociology*, there is a reference to HT384 for works about a specific region or country. The schedule says to Cutter by region or country. The first Cutter (.x) is for general works; the second (.x2), Local, A-Z. Since this is a general work, the first Cutter is .G7, the second is for the author, Williamson. If the book were about Manchester, the first Cutter would be .G72 and the second would be M38. Of the M38, the M3 is for Manchester and the 8 for Williamson (Manual G 060). There are only two Cutters per call number as a general rule; some map numbers call for three.

Dewey Classification: Under "Cities" in the index, the subdivision "Sociology" is the one appropriate to this book. It refers to 307.76. In the schedule .7609 is used for historical and geographic treatment. In the geographic area tables, -41 is used for the British Isles. To this may be added a subdivision for the historical periods. The notation for the nineteenth century is -09034.

EXAMPLE 13

TITLE PAGE

> Santa Cruz County/City Law Enforcement
>
> # Helicopter Patrol Program
>
> **Prepared by**
>
> Research, Planning and Development Unit
> Administration Division
> Santa Cruz Police Department
>
> **In Cooperation with the**
>
> Santa Cruz County Sheriff's Department
> and Other Cities and Agencies in the County
>
> April 1, 1973

OTHER INFORMATION

The introduction includes the statement:

> The objectives of this report are to illustrate the effectiveness of helicopter patrol as a proven means of crime suppression and to identify alternative plans for its utilization in the combined cities and county of Santa Cruz.

WORKSHEET

09—

650

090	HV8080.A3 $b S35 1973
092 0	363.2320979471 $b S231 $2 20
650 0	Aeronautics in police work $z California $z Santa Cruz County.

The topic of the book is the use of helicopter patrols by the police forces of Santa Cruz County, California.

Subject headings: If the cataloger begins with the term *Helicopter* in LCSH, he or she will not find any headings such as *Helicopters in police work* or *in law enforcement*. Under *Patrols* there is a reference to *Guard duty*. A scan of the headings beginning with *Police* eventually leads to *Police patrols*, which has a reference to a narrower term *Aeronautics in police work*. This is the most specific heading available. It may be subdivided geographically.

LC Classification: The subject heading chosen for this book has a reference to class number HV8080.A3. In *Class H: Subclasses HM-HX: Social Sciences: Sociology*, HV8080 is for "Other police duties and methods of protection, A-Z" and .A3 is for "Aeronautics in police work."

Dewey Classification: There are no appropriate numbers under "Aeronautics" in the index. The term "Police patrols" refers to 363.232. This is the most appropriate number for the book. To it the geographic area notation for Santa Cruz County may be added. Since there is no other provision for standard subdivisions, the notation -09 is added, followed by -79471 from Table 2.

EXAMPLE 14

TITLE PAGE

> # Music for Brass Instruments
>
> ### For 2 Trumpets in B-flat, Horn in F, 2 Trombones
>
> Ingolf Dahl
>
> New York : Warner Bros., 1949

OTHER INFORMATION The music consists of a score plus a separate part for each player.

WORKSHEET 09__

650

090		M557.4.D22 $b M8 1949
092	0	785.9195 $b D131m $2 20
650	0	Brass quintets (Horn, trombones (2), trumpets (2)) $x Scores and parts.

The music consists of a score and set of parts of a quintet for brass instruments.

Subject headings: A brief explanation of the method LCSH uses to create headings for instrumental ensembles is included in the Introduction, p. xvi-xvii. It is clear that the first essential step is to determine the number of parts for instrumental music. When there are three to nine parts, the terms *Trios* to *Nonets* are used. When all the instruments are from one "family," the terms *String quartet, Brass sextet, Woodwind quintet, etc.* are used. If the cataloger begins at the term *Quintet*, LCSH includes a reference from *Quintets, Brass* to *Brass quintets*. The instrumentation for such ensembles is then specified according to the scope note. The actual heading needed appears in the list, but, if it did not, it could be constructed by the cataloger. The form subdivision is added following Section H 1160 of the Manual.

LC Classification: LCSH refers from the subject headings used for this score to *M555-559* in *Class M: Music and Books on Music*. In the schedule, a footnote says that the span of numbers is subarranged like M355-559. The number for separate works for trios of brass instruments only is 357.4; so, for quintets it is 557.4.

Dewey Classification: The index has an entry for "Quintets, chamber music" that refers to 785.15. This number is too general since it does not specify the types of instruments. There is also an entry for "Brass chamber ensembles" that refers to 785.9. The schedules include directions to add to that number as instructed under 785.2-785.9. Under that heading for "Specific kinds of ensembles" are directions for adding notation for general principles, musical forms, and size of ensemble. The cataloger is instructed to add -19 to indicate size. Then the schedule says to add to 19 the numbers following 785.1 in 785.12-785.19. In that sequence, 2 is used for duets, 3 for trios, etc. So -195 is added since this work is a quintet. A letter for the title has been included in the completed call number because in music it is more the rule than the exception that there is more than one work by a given author in a given class number.

EXAMPLE 15

TITLE PAGE

> # Timor, Chants des Ema
>
> France : Chants du Monde, 1979

OTHER INFORMATION

This is a field recording of songs of the Ema people made on Timor in 1966 and 1969-1970.

WORKSHEET

09__

650

650

650

090		M1824.I5 $b T5 1979
092	0	781.629922 $b T585 $2 20
650	0	Kemak (Indonesian people) $x Music.
650	0	Folk music $z Indonesia $z Timor Island.
650	0	Folk-songs, Kemak $z Indonesia $z Timor Island.

This recording consists of folk songs sung by the Ema of Timor.

Subject headings: Section H 1917 of the Manual gives instruction for providing the subject headings for music of ethnic and national groups. Of the headings specified there, the following are appropriate for this work:

1 Ethnic or national group—[place]—Music.
2 [heading(s) for musical genre or style, or for ballads and songs with national emphasis]
3 [heading(s) for language, i.e. *Ballads, Folk-songs,* or *Songs* with language qualifier]

The first heading should be for the Ema, subdivided by place and with the form subdivision *Music*. The term *Ema* in LCSH refers to *Kemak (Indonesian people)*. Since the name of the ethnic group includes the name of the place, the geographic subdivision can be omitted as redundant. The next heading is for the genre *Folk music* with a geographic subdivision for Timor. The authorized form of *Timor* is *Timor Island (Indonesia)*, which becomes *Indonesia—Timor Island* as an indirect subdivision, in accordance with Section H 807 of the Manual ("Islands in Indirect Subdivision Practice.") The last heading is to include the language. Following the entry for the Kemak is one for *Kemak language*. Thus the language of the songs can be assumed to be Kemak; so the entry is *Folk-songs, Kemak* with the geographical subdivision.

LC Classification: Many libraries do not classify sound recordings. The classification is included here since it is the same as for printed music. The index of *Class M: Music and Books on Music* does not include the term Kemak, and Indonesia refers only to books on Indonesian music. The class outline lists M1627-1853 for *National music*. Under Asia, there is no specific number for Indonesia. So it will be classified under 1824 or 1825 which are to be used for other regions or countries. A footnote says "Subarranged like 1684-1685." The number 1684 is used for collections; 1685, for separate works. Since this is a collection of songs, M1824 is the appropriate number with the first Cutter for Indonesia.

Dewey Classification: In the index the term "Folk music" refers to 781.62. The schedules say to add to 781.62 national or ethnic group notation 1-9 from table 5. Indonesia is -9922.

EXAMPLE 16

TITLE PAGE

El Greco to Murillo

Spanish Painting in the Golden Age, 1556-1700

Nina Ayala Mallory

New York : HarperCollins Publishers, © 1990

OTHER INFORMATION

Text from the dust jacket includes:

This thorough survey of one of the great periods of Western art includes such masters as El Greco, Ribera, Zurbaran, Velazquez, Murillo, and others. The book concentrates on the two main artistic centers in Spain during the seventeenth century—Seville and Madrid. The major figures and their works are studied in depth and the secondary figures in the context of their respective schools. The art and artists are studied in relation to the historical and cultural environment in Spain from the reign of Philip II through Charles II. The development of Spanish art in their period is covered chronologically, and the uniqueness of Spanish art and its relationship to Renaissance and Baroque Italian and Flemish art is explained.

WORKSHEET

09__

650

650

650

090		ND805 $b .M35 1990
092	0	759.609032 $b M255 $2 20
650	0	Painting, Spanish.
650	0	Painting $y 16th century $z Spain.
650	0	Painting, Modern $y 17th-18th centuries $z Spain.

The topic of this book is Spanish painting from 1556 to 1700.

Subject Headings: LCSH does not have a cross reference from *Spanish painting* to the used term *Painting, Spanish*. There is, however, a cross reference from *Spanish art* to the used term *Art, Spanish,* which is suggestive that the related used term might also be an inverted term. For the books about art, Section H 1250 of the Manual says "the subject cataloger normally assigns a set of headings to a work being cataloged rather than a single heading." For books on works of art by more than one artist, the Manual prescribes headings to bring out the *[art form], [national, ethnic or religious background]—[place of origin],* and the *[art form with period qualifier and/or country subdivision]—[place of origin].* Other types of headings are also prescribed but are not appropriate for this particular work. *Painting, Spanish* is not subdivided with period subdivisions, so the additional headings are needed to cover the period dealt with in the book.

LC Classification: LCSH does not suggest a class number for Spanish painting, and the index for *Class N: Fine Arts* has no entry under "Painting, Spanish" or "Spanish painting." The index does list: "Painting: ND . . . History: ND49-1113." Scanning this part of the schedule, one finds that the history of painting in special countries is classified in ND201-1114, and that Table IV is to be used. A footnote says to "Add country number in table to 200." The range of numbers in Table IV for Spain is 601-613.3. One adds 200 and the range becomes 801-813.3, which is to be divided like 341-353.3. In the range 341-353.3, there is no single number that covers the 16th-18th centuries, so one selects the number for the first century covered in the book, i.e. the 16th century. This number is 345. Therefore, ND805 is the appropriate number.

Dewey Classification: The index has no listing under "Painting, Spanish" or "Spanish painting," but does list "Painting, Arts 750." In the schedule, the note under "750 Painting and paintings" says to classify works with geographical treatment in 759.1-.9. The number for Spain is in the range 759.3-.8, for "Other European countries." Here the cataloger is directed to "add to the base number 759 the numbers following -4 in notation 43-48 from Table 2." Table 2 assigns Spain the number 46, so we add 6 to 759 (759.6). To this number, we then add a number for the historical period from Table 1, Standard Subdivisions. The number 09032 for "17th century, 1600-1699" comes closest to covering the period dealt with in the book.

EXAMPLE 17

TITLE PAGE

Those Fabulous Serial Heroines

Their Lives and Films

by

Buck Rainey

Metuchen, N.J. : The Scarecrow Press, Inc., 1990

OTHER INFORMATION

Text from the introduction:

> The demise of the serial leaves the older generation of moviegoers with a sense of moroseness. An important part of our lives has disappeared. Mountains of prose have been written about this action genre, expressing the height and depth, the length and breadth of one's affection for it.
>
> Motion picture serials depended for their survival on thrills, stunts, death-defying acrobatics, speed, hokum, minimum dialogue, childish plots, unsophisticated audiences, and various other elements, but in nearly every case there had to be a beautiful girl in jeopardy.
>
> This book is about a number of the more important serial heroines who were loved, supported, and fantasized about by three generations of action fans. The filmographies will be a boon to film historians and fans who have always wanted a fairly complete filmography of their favorite heroine. Many readers will be more interested in the biographical data and the photographs.

WORKSHEET

09__

650

650

```
090        PN1998.2 $b .R35 1990

092 0      791.430280922 $b R156 $2 20
```

650 0 Motion picture actors and actresses $z United States $x Biography.

650 0 Motion picture serials.

The topic of the book is actresses in motion picture serials.

Subject headings: In LCSH *Actresses* refers also to a narrower term *Motion picture actors and actresses*. The heading allows for geographical subdivision, and, since these are American movies, *United States* is added as a subdivision. Even though the heading by itself might seem to imply that this is a biography, there are actually more than two hundred free-floating subdivisions from *Abstracting and indexing* to *Wounds and injuries* in Section H 1095 of the Manual that may be added to a heading for a class of persons. In this case, the subdivision *Biography* must be added. In LCSH, there is a reference from *Serials, Motion picture* to *Motion picture serials*. Together these two headings encompass the subject of this book.

LC Classification: In the index *Class P: Subclasses PN, PR, PS, PZ: Literature (General), English and American Literature, Fiction in English, Juvenile Belles Lettres*, "Motion pictures" refers to PN1993+. PN1995.9.S3 is for Serials; PN1998.2 is for collective biography. Both numbers include part of the topic of the book but are each more general. There is no guidance in the schedule as to which to prefer; so the cataloger must arbitrarily choose one.

Dewey Classification: In the index, the term "Actors" has a subdivision "Motion pictures" which refers to 791.43028092. That number does not appear in the schedules. The standard subdivisions are to be applied to 791.43, the number for motion pictures, as modified under 792.01-.09. Under that number -028 is used for acting and performance. The standard subdivision -092 is for biography; in this case -0922 is used for group biography.

EXAMPLE 18

TITLE PAGE

> # The Lives and Times of Ebenezer Scrooge
>
> Paul Davis
>
> New Haven : Yale University Press, © 1990

OTHER INFORMATION

Text from the dust jacket:

"Bah! Humbug!" and "God bless us, every one!" are phrases that have resounded through the years, instantly recognizable as exclamations from Scrooge and Tiny Tim in Charles Dickens's beloved *Christmas Carol*. Told and retold to generations of children and adults, *A Christmas Carol* has been adapted, revised, condensed, added to, and modernized more than any other work in English literature. In this engaging and delightfully illustrated book, Paul Davis explores the various British and American versions of this work—on stage, film, radio, and television and in literature, cartoon, and comic books—showing how these interpretations have reflected the changing cultural perspectives of successive eras.

According to Davis, six periods have shaped this cultural history, each contributing to the evolving culture-text of *A Christmas Carol* that is what we remember of all its parodies, piracies, and retellings. Dicken's original story, written in 1843, provided proof that urbanization had not destroyed Christmas and that the old country traditions could flourish in the new cities. By the 1870s, *A Christmas Carol* had become secular scripture, read as a retelling of the biblical story. The sophisticated decade preceding World War I treated the work for the first time as a story for children. In the Depression era, while the British reaffirmed a traditional *Carol*, Americans interpreted Scrooge's transformation as the triumph of a new business ethic of service and sharing. The Scrooge of the 1960s became a Freudian figure tormented by his past, who conjured up Marley as a way of calling for help and who turned on to Christmas and tuned into the joys he had denied himself. Now, when our focus is on hunger and homelessness rather than joy in the streets, Scrooge is again a social figure placed in the center of unsettling economic realities.

WORKSHEET

09__
600
600
600
650

090		PR4572.C7 $b D38 1990
092	0	823.8 $b D548czD263 $2 20
600	10	Dickens, Charles, $d 1812-1870. $t Christmas carol.
600	10	Dickens, Charles, $d 1812-1870 $x Adaptations.
600	10	Dickens, Charles, $d 1812-1870 $x Characters $x Ebenezer Scrooge.
650	0	Scrooge, Ebenezer (Fictious character)

This book is about *A Christmas Carol* by Charles Dickens, about the ways in which it has been adapted, and about the character in the book Ebenezer Scrooge.

Subject headings: When one work is criticism of another, the first subject heading is an entry for the work being written about. The form of the subject entry is determined by the rules for descriptive cataloging in *AACR2*, in this case a name-title added entry. Section H 1155.4 of the Manual provides a list of subdivisions that may be used under the names of individual literary authors. The terms from that list that are appropriate to this work are *Adaptations* and *Characters—[Name of character]*. This work includes information about the ways *Christmas Carol* has been "adapted, revised, condensed, added to and modernized." Thus the subdivision *Adaptations* is added to Dickens' name. While this work concerns only adaptations of *A Christmas Carol*, there is no provision for adding the subdivision to a name-title heading. Since there is material about Scrooge particularly, the subdivision *Characters—Ebenezer Scrooge* is used. There can also be an added entry for Scrooge himself. Section H 1610 of the Manual gives directions for making entries for fictitious characters: "Establish in inverted form all characters whose names include a surname . . . Add the parenthetical qualifier *(Fictitious character)*." These headings are tagged 650, i.e., as topical headings, not personal names.

LC Classification: *Class P: Subclasses PN, PR, PS, PZ: Literature (General), English and American Literature, Fiction in English, Juvenile Belles Lettres* includes 49 numbers for Dickens, PR4550-4598. Works about a literary work are classified to follow directly after the work. There is no individual number for *A Christmas Carol*; so it is classified in PR4572 which is for "Other [works] A-Z." For criticism of an individual work, Table XXXI (Authors with 49 numbers) refers to Table XLIII (Separate Works with Successive Cutter numbers). This table instructs the cataloger to use the third Cutter for criticism and to arrange the criticism A-Z by main entry of the work. In this case the Cutters LC has used are C68, C69, and C7; so the third Cutter is C7. The Cutter for Davis is D38.

Dewey Classification: The entry for "English literature" in the index refers to 820. English fiction is classified in 823. Period tables at the beginning of the 820s call for .8 to be added for the Victorian period. A work letter has been added to the Cutter for the title of the *Christmas Carol*, and the letter *z* is added to that to indicate that this is criticism of that work. Then a second Cutter is added for the author of the criticism.

EXAMPLE 19

TITLE PAGE

> # Writing Effective Software Documentation
>
> Patricia A. Williams
>
> Pamela S. Beason
>
> Glenview, Illinois : Scott, Foresman and Company, 1990

OTHER INFORMATION

The introduction states:

Writing Effective Software Documentation is for anyone who has to write documentation that explains software applications, systems, and languages to users, including:

- independent programmers who develop software to sell to the general public or on contract for companies
- programmers who develop software for their companies
- systems analysts and systems engineers who oversee the development of software for their companies
- technical writers who document software for companies

No matter what kind of documentation you need to write, this book

- shows you how to use predeveloped forms during software development to record information that will serve as a basis for your documentation
- tells you how to plan and manage a documentation project
- clarifies the types of documentation you should use to reach different kinds of users and achieve different types of goals
- shows you how to organize each type of documentation
- gives you concrete writing techniques to make your documents easy to read
- shows you excerpts from existing documentation to use as models

WORKSHEET

09—
650
650

090   QA76.9.D6 $b W55 1990

092 0   005.15 $b W726 $2 20

650 0   Electronic data processing documentation.

650 0   Computer software $x Development.

This book is about writing the documentation for computer software.

Subject Headings: Under the entry *Software, Computer* in LCSH is a reference to *Computer software*. The list of subdivisions includes *Development* but not *Documentation*. *Computer software—Development* is assigned as a heading because writing the documentation for software is part of its development. When LCSH is approached from the term *Documentation*, after a list of related terms, there is a reference from *Documentation in electronic data processing* to *Electronic data processing documentation*. That then is the heading that best encompasses the subject of software documentation.

LC Classification: Since computer science is included in *Class Q: Science*, the first place to look for the correct class number is in the index to the Q schedule. Under "Computer software" is a reference to QA76.75+, but nothing in the list of special topics under software applies to documentation. Another look in the index under "Documentation in computer science" leads to QA76.9.D6, which is the most appropriate number.

Dewey Classification: In the index there is no entry under "Documentation". There are entries under "Computer software" and "Computer programming." The number for software, 005.3, looks like it could be appropriate since it can be used for the topic "documentation." However, under 005.1, "Computer programming," the number 005.15 is provided for preparation of program documentation.

EXAMPLE 20

TITLE PAGE

Large Lakes

Ecological Structure and Function

Max M. Tilzer
Colette Serruya

(editors)

Berlin : Springer-Verlag, 1990

OTHER INFORMATION

Text from the foreword includes:

> Although in principle water is a "renewable resource," the world's water reserves are diminishing in two fashions, the effects of which are multiplicative: enhanced consumption and accelerated degradation of quality.... This volume... considers large lakes as objects of scientific curiosity, as study sites for physicists, geochemists, and a wide array of biologists. These scientists have a common vision of large lakes as huge reactors, in which physical, chemical, and biological processes interact closely and in an extremely complex fashion.... Only if the processes in a "healthy" ecosystem are properly understood, will we be able to successfully attack the formidable challenge of maintaining or, if necessary, restoring their quality.... The contributions to this volume were the product of a symposium....

WORKSHEET

09—

650

090   QH541.5.L3 $b L35 1990

092 0   574.526332 $b L332 $2 20

650 0   Lake ecology $x Congresses.

The topic of this book is the ecology of lakes.

Subject Headings: *Lakes* is a used term in LCSH. Under that term, the narrower term *Lake ecology* is listed as a used term. This single heading exactly covers the subject of the book. Section H 1095 of the Manual lists *Congresses* as a free-floating subdivision used for collections of papers that result from a symposium or conference.

LC Classification: Under the heading *Lake ecology* in LCSH, the number QH541.5.L3 is given. This is a case in which the number suggested in LCSH is precisely the correct class number for the work being cataloged. The index to *Class Q: Science* also cites this number under the entry "Lakes: Ecology."

Dewey Classification: The index contains the entry "Lake ecology 574.526 332." The schedule confirms that this class number is appropriate and complete.

EXAMPLE 21

TITLE PAGE

Fire in North American Tallgrass Prairies

Edited by

Scott L. Collins and Linda L. Wallace

Norman and London : University of Oklahoma Press 1990

OTHER INFORMATION

Text from the dust jacket includes:

> The authors . . . concentrate on the effects of fire in several spatial and temporal dimensions, including individual plants and animal populations, plant and animal communities, ecosystem functions, and landscape processes. Based on papers presented at a 1987 symposium . . . this book represents an important contribution to key unanswered questions concerning the role of fire in grassland ecosystems . . . .

From the table of contents:

> Fire as a Natural Disturbance in Tallgrass Prairie Ecosystems
> Fire in North American Grasslands: A Historical Perspective
> Photosynthesis and Leaf Area Development of *Andropogon Gerardii* in Response to Fire
> Fire in Central North American Grasslands: Vegetative Reproduction, Seed Germination, and Seedling Establishment
> Mammals and Grassland Fires
> Effects of Fire on Plant Community Structure in Prairies
> Stimulating the Interactive Impact of Fire and Grazing on C, N, and P Cycling in a Tallgrass Prairie
> Fire in North American Tallgrass Prairies: A Landscape Perspective

WORKSHEET

09__

650

650

650

```
090      QK110 $b .F57 1990

092 0    574.52643   $b F523 $2 20

650 0    Prairie ecology $z North America $x Congresses.

650 0    Grassland fires $x Environmental aspects $z North
         America $x Congresses.

650 0    Fire ecology $z North America $x Congresses.
```

The topic of this book is the ecological effects of fire in the tallgrass prairies of North America.

Subject Headings: Examination of the table of a contents reveals that the focus of the articles is primarily on plant rather than animal ecology: only one article deals with mammals.

LCSH lists the used term *Fire*. Under this term, one finds *Environmental aspects* USE *Fire ecology*. To the heading *Fire ecology*, we add the geographical subdivision *North America*. It is already clear that we cannot cover all aspects of the topic in one topical heading. *Fire ecology* does not cover the other topical words "Tallgrass" and "Prairies." Under *Fire ecology* we find a broader term, *Grassland fires*, that looks promising. But first we continue searching directly under the remaining words taken directly from the book's title.

Neither "tallgrass" nor "tall grass" are used terms in LCSH, nor is there a reference from either of those terms. Scanning the headings beginning with *Grass*, we find *Grasses*. But the terms for which *Grasses* is the used term—i.e., Agrostology, Graminaceae, Gramineae, etc.—do not seem relevant to our book. Nor are any of the narrower or broader terms listed under *Grasses* relevant. A little further in the list, one finds *Grassland ecology, Grassland fires,* and *Grasslands,* all of which may be subdivided geographically. *Grassland fires* is the one that most closely corresponds to the topic of the book. The free-floating subdivision *Environmental aspects*, listed in Section H 1095 of the Manual, is added to the heading so it more precisely matches the topic of the book. (Since fire is a "process," *Grassland fires* qualifies to have this subdivision added to it.) According to Section H 860, this subdivision may be further subdivided by place, so *North America* is then added to the heading.

Prairies is a used term, which includes a see also reference to headings beginning with the word *Prairie*. Scanning the latter headings, one finds *Prairie ecology*, which is closer than *Prairies* is to the specific topic of the book. *Prairie ecology* may be subdivided geographically, so *North America* should be added to the heading.

In accord with Section H 180 of the Manual, the free-floating subdivision *Congresses* is added to each of the topical headings.

LC Classification: Of the three headings selected, *Prairie ecology—North America—Congresses* is the most comprehensive in relation to the book, and so will be listed first. In LCSH, the number QH541.5.P7 is listed with *Prairie ecology*. There are no LC Class numbers listed with *Fire ecology* and *Grassland fires*. In the index to *Class Q: Science,* we find:

> Prairies
>   Ecology: QH541.5.P7
>   Natural history: QK87.7
>   Plant ecology: QK938.P7

The first number listed, QH541.5.P7, looks promising but is not appropriate because the scope note for "QH540: Ecology" says "Class here works concerned with general and animal ecology . . . for plant ecology, *see* QK901+." The third number listed in the index, QK938.P7, would therefore seem appropriate. But, QK938.P7 is under "Botany: Plant ecology: Physiographic regions (General)," whereas our book is about North America only. There is a note at the end of QK938 which says "Topographical divisions, *see* QK108+." Also, near the beginning of the section "QK900 Plant Ecology," we see a note that says "(903) Ecological discussion of areas, *see* QK108+." Under "QK108 Botany: Topographical divisions," we find "QK110 North America," which is the appropriate LC class number for the book.

Dewey Classification: The index lists "Prairie ecology 574.526 43." The index also lists this same number under "Grassland ecology." There is no listing in the index for "Fire ecology," but there is one under "Fire, ecological effect 574.522 2."

Examination of both numbers in the schedule reveals that either one might seem appropriate. The Introduction to the DDC gives the following among its guidelines for classifying works on more than one subject:

> Class a work dealing with interrelated subjects with the subject being acted upon. [Vol. 1, p. xxxi]

In this case, fire is acting upon grasslands, so the first number, "574.52643 Grasslands, meadows, prairies" is the correct choice.

EXAMPLE 22

TITLE PAGE

Descriptive Cataloging For the AACR2R and USMARC

Larry Millsap and Terry Ellen Ferl

Santa Cruz: University Library,
University of California, 1990

OTHER INFORMATION

Text from the preface includes:

> This workbook is designed to give catalogers practice in creating original descriptive cataloging records which can be shared with other libraries in an automated environment . . . . Bibliographic information is presented in a series of exercises which require application of cataloging rules and machine-readable coding conventions common to the cataloging community . . . . The essential tools for creating original descriptive cataloging records in machine-readable form are the *Anglo-American Cataloguing Rules,* 2nd ed. 1988 Revision *(AACR2R),* and the *USMARC Format for Bibliographic Data.*

From the table of contents:

> Part I. Introduction to the Rules
> Part II. Machine-Readable Format
> Part III. The Exercises

WORKSHEET

09__
650
630
650

090		Z694.15.A56 $b M55 1990
092	0	025.32076 $b M657 $2 20
650	0	Descriptive cataloging $x Rules $x Problems, exercises, etc.
630	00	Anglo-American cataloguing rules.
650	0	MARC System $z United States $x Format $x Problems, exercises, etc.

This is a workbook for practice in preparing descriptive cataloging records based on *AACR2R* with machine-readable coding according to the USMARC format.

Subject Headings: In LCSH, *Descriptive cataloging* is a used term, and the subdivision *Rules* appears under it. There is no term in LCSH under "workbooks," but under *Exercises, Practice,* one finds a directive to use the *subdivision Problems, exercises, etc. under topical headings for compilations of practice problems or exercises pertinent to the study of a particular subject.* A subject heading for the uniform title of the cataloging code is added in accord with Section H 180 of the Manual, because it is significant for the work as a whole. There is no listing in LCSH under *USMARC,* but under the listing *Machine-readable catalog system,* there is a cross reference to *MARC System,* which is subdivided geographically. The used subdivision *Format* may then be added, followed by the form subdivision *Problems, exercises, etc.*

LC Classification: The class number Z694 is suggested in LCSH under the subject heading *Descriptive cataloging.* In *Class Z: Bibliography and Library Science,* this number contains a breakdown "By system, A-Z" under Z694.15. The Cutter number .A56 is assigned to the "Anglo-American cataloguing rules, 2d ed., 1978 (AACR 2)." As of June 1990, no number for the 1988 revision of the second edition has been published, so this number will be used for the work.

Dewey Classification: The index lists "Descriptive cataloging 025.32," and the schedule confirms that this number is used for "descriptive-cataloging codes, e.g., Anglo-American Cataloguing Rules." To bring out the form of this related work (a book of exercises), 076 from Table 1 is added to the base number. The index does contain the listing "Exercises (Education) T1-076," which serves as entry to the Table.

3 SELECTED BIBLIOGRAPHY

BASIC SOURCES

Library of Congress. Subject Cataloging Division. *Library of Congress Subject Headings.* 14th ed. Washington, D.C.: Cataloging Distribution Service, Library of Congress, 1991.

> The well-known "red book," also called *LCSH,* currently consists of three bound volumes. New editions are available annually, by subscription. *LCSH* is also available as *Library of Congress Subject Headings Cumulative Microform Edition,* which provides the equivalent of a new edition each quarter. Another version, *CDMARC Subjects,* provides a quarterly cumulated compact disc with the entire *LCSH* file. Prices for 1990 in each format are: $150.00 (book), $80.00 (microfiche), and $300.00 (compact disc). *CDMARC Subjects* requires an IBM PC (XT/AT or compatible), 640K RAM, DOS 3.1 or higher, a CD-ROM reader conforming to the High Sierra standard, and a CD-ROM driver which uses Microsoft extensions.

Library of Congress. Office for Subject Cataloging Policy. *Subject Cataloging Manual: Subject Headings.* Washington, D.C.: Cataloging Distribution Service, Library of Congress, 1990.

> This two-volume, loose-leaf publication is the third edition. LC issues updates periodically. This work is essential for consistent application of *LCSH.* The 1990 subscription price, including updates, is $110.00.

Library of Congress. Office for Subject Cataloging Policy. *Free-floating Subdivisions: an Alphabetical Index.* 2nd ed. Washington, D.C.: Cataloging Distribution Service, Library of Congress, 1990.

> This manual is a single source listing of every free-floating subdivision in the Library of Congress subject heading system. It includes references to memoranda in the *Subject Cataloging Manual,* and is designed to serve as an index to that tool.

LC Classification Schedules.

> This set of 45 schedules devised by the Library of Congress consists of separate volumes for classes A through Z of the LC classification system. Available from LC, the individual schedules range in price from a few dollars to $20.00. They are kept up-to-date by the quarterly publication *LC Classification—Additions and Changes,* available from LC on subscription for $80.00 a year.

> A boon to catalogers involved in a substantial amount of original cataloging and classification are the so-called "Gale Cums." These publications periodically consolidate the quarterly LC *Additions and Changes* so that catalogers can verify classification numbers in only one or two lookups. Annually, Gale Research Inc. integrates the latest edition of each LC classification schedule with all of LC's *Additions and Changes* published to date and reissues them. The 1990 cost of a full set of the classification

schedules combined with the cumulated additions and changes was nearly $5,000 (microfiche, about $3,000). For libraries that already own the LC editions of the schedules, a set of the cumulated *Additions and Changes* alone costs about $2,600 (microfiche about $1,600). Schedules and cumulations may also be purchased individually from Gale.

Library of Congress. Subject Cataloging Division. *Subject Cataloging Manual: Shelflisting*. Washington, D.C.: Subject Cataloging Division, Library of Congress, 1987.

This is a manual for catalogers who wish to complete LC call numbers according to LC policy and practice. It describes procedures for assigning Cutter numbers in many different shelflisting situations. The 1990 price was $30.00.

Dewey, Melvil. *Dewey Decimal Classification and Relative Index*. Edition 20. Albany, N.Y.: Forest Press, a Division of OCLC Online Computer Library Center, 1989.

The 20th edition is a four-volume work, which costs $225.00. Volume 1 contains a concise and essential introduction to the DDC, and the text of the auxiliary Tables used in number building, e.g., Table 1, Standard Subdivisions; Table 2, Geographic Areas, Historical Periods, Persons; etc. Volume 2 contains Schedules 000-599; volume 3, Schedules 600-999. Summaries, which are outlines of the Schedules, are printed at the beginning of volumes 2 and 3. Volume 4 contains the Relative Index and the Manual. The Manual, which comprises nearly one-third of volume 4, is published for the first time as part of the Dewey Schedules. It contains notes about usage of the Tables and Schedule Numbers, and some flow charts that help build numbers in complex portions of the Schedules.

Á The 12th edition of the *Abridged Dewey Decimal Classification and Relative Index* was published in 1990. This single-volume (857 pp.) work may be more appropriate than the full edition for most small and medium-sized libraries.

C.A. *Cutter's Alfabetic-Order Table—Consonants, Except S and Vowels and S*. Altered and fitted with three figures by Miss Kate E. Sanborn. [Boston: Library Bureau, 1896?]

The Cutter-Sanborn tables may be used to create book numbers for works classified in the Dewey classification system. As described by Donald Lehnus in the work cited below (p. 142), this 1896 edition of the tables combines into one physical volume the consonants and vowels of the Cutter-Sanborn tables, which were originally published in separate volumes. The introduction to DDC 20 (vol. 1, p. xlix-l) states that the Cutter-Sanborn tables are available from Libraries Unlimited, Littleton, Colorado.

USMARC Concise Format for Bibliographic, Authority, and Holdings Data. Prepared by Network Development and MARC Standards Office. Washington: Cataloging Distribution Service, Library of Congress, 1988.

> An inexpensive, single-volume work that provides a *concise* description of USMARC. Describes each field, each character position of the fixed-length data element fields, and the indicators in the variable data fields. The full text of USMARC is published as *USMARC Format for Bibliographic Data Including Guidelines for Content Designation*. Both the full document and the concise version are kept up-to-date by the periodic issuing of new and replacement pages. In order to describe an item and enter it into a computerized system, a cataloging agency will need to consult the documentation of the cataloging utility or system to which records are contributed. This documentation will include manuals for tagging and coding records in USMARC-based formats.

AUXILIARY SOURCES

Bilindex: A Bilingual Spanish-English Subject Heading List: Spanish Equivalents to Library of Congress Subject Headings. Oakland, Calif.: California Spanish Language Data Base, 1984.

> Based on the 9th edition of LCSH, this thesaurus and its supplements provide standardized Spanish-language terminology for subject access. This cataloging tool allows libraries to enhance catalog and subject access to Spanish and bilingual collections. The list provides access for regional variants of authorized Spanish subject terms (e.g., Latin American, Peninsular, Southwestern, Cuban, Mexican, Mexican-American or Chicano, and Puerto Rican usage).

Chan, Lois Mai. *Library of Congress Subject Headings: Principles and Application.* 2nd ed. Littleton, Colo.: Libraries Unlimited, 1986.

> This book covers the historical development of the LC subject heading system, the principles that support it, its application at LC, and its viability in online retrieval. Included are several bibliographies useful for those who wish to study particular issues in subject cataloging.

Chan, Lois Mai. *Immroth's Guide to the Library of Congress Classification.* 4th ed. Littleton, Colo.: Libraries Unlimited, 1990.

> This work provides the cataloger with basic understanding of the characteristics of the LC classification system, the arrangement within the classes, the format of the schedules and tables, and special problems of use.

Lehnus, Donald J. *Book Numbers: History, Principles, and Application.* Chicago: American Library Association, 1980.

> A comprehensive work on the origins and development of book numbers, particularly the Cutter Tables, in the 19th and 20th centuries. This work

may also be consulted by catalogers who need to expand book numbers beyond the standard tables.

Miksa, Francis. *The Subject in the Dictionary Catalog from Cutter to the Present*. Chicago: American Library Association, 1983.

In this scholarly work, the author explains Charles Ammi Cutter's subject heading system, and the developments in subject heading systems since Cutter.

Terry Ellen Ferl is Principal Cataloger, University of California, Santa Cruz.

Larry Millsap is Head, Bibliographic Records Section, and Acting Head, Reference Services Section, University of California, Santa Cruz.

Book design: Gloria Brown
Cover design: Gregory Apicella
Typography: Roberts/Churcher

MLib-TechServices